W9-CPF-685

EASY ORIGAMI
JUNGLE ANIMALS

An Augmented Reading Paper Folding Experience

BY
JOHN MONTROLL

CAPSTONE PRESS
a capstone imprint

TABLE OF CONTENTS

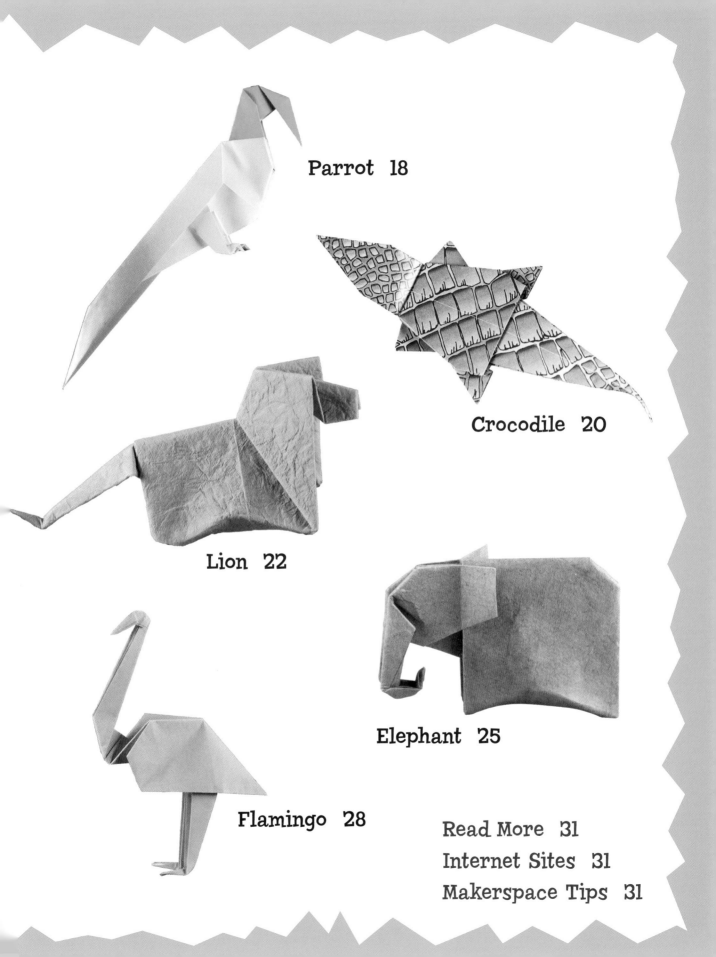

ORIGAMI SAFARI

Journey into the jungle! On this paper-folding adventure, you'll fold parrots, peacocks, crocodiles, gorillas, and so much more!

Best of all, every model in this book is easy to fold. Simple instructions and diagrams walk you through every step. And if you get stuck, just watch the Capstone 4D videos. They'll show you each fold in action.

So grab some paper squares and flex your fingers. Your origami safari starts now!

Download the Capstone  app!

- Ask an adult to download the Capstone 4D app.
- Scan the cover and stars inside the book for additional content.

When you scan a spread, you'll find fun extra stuff to go with this book! You can also find these things on the web at www.capstone4D.com using the password: jungle.13066

SYMBOLS

Lines

— — — — — — — — —   Valley fold, fold in front.

—·—·—·—·—·—   Mountain fold, fold behind.

—————————   Crease line.

··················   X-ray or guide line.

Arrows

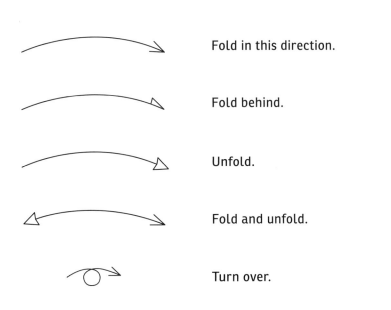

Fold in this direction.

Fold behind.

Unfold.

Fold and unfold.

Turn over.

Sink or three dimensional folding.

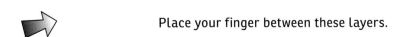

Place your finger between these layers.

5

BASIC FOLDS ★

Pleat Fold

Fold back and forth. Each pleat is composed of one valley and mountain fold. Here are two examples.

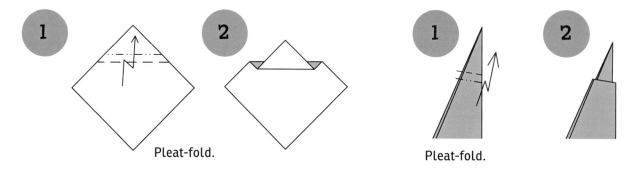

Pleat-fold.

Pleat-fold.

Squash Fold

In a squash fold, some paper is opened and then made flat. The shaded arrow shows where to place your finger.

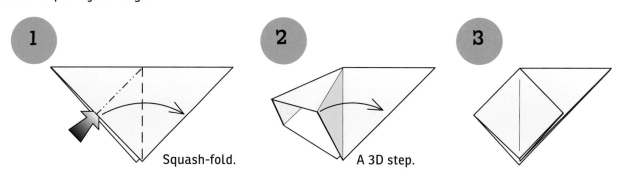

Squash-fold.

A 3D step.

Rabbit Ear

To fold a rabbit ear, one corner is folded in half and laid down to a side.

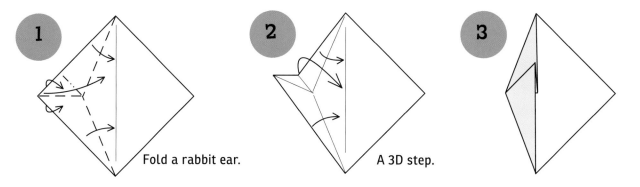

Fold a rabbit ear.

A 3D step.

6

Inside Reverse Fold

In an inside reverse fold, some paper is folded between layers. Here are two examples.

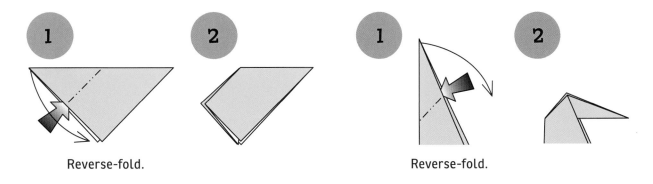

Reverse-fold.   Reverse-fold.

Outside Reverse Fold

Much of the paper must be unfolded to make an outside reverse fold.

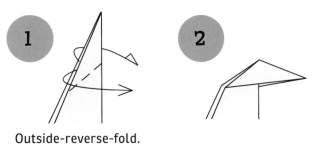

Outside-reverse-fold.

Crimp Fold

A crimp fold is a combination of two reverse folds. Open the model slightly to form the crimp evenly on each side. Here are two examples.

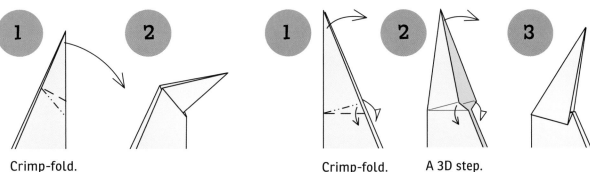

Crimp-fold.   Crimp-fold.   A 3D step.

BAT ★

On a moonlit summer night
A pair of wings have taken flight.
They swoop beneath the canopy
Dodging every vine and tree.
This bat will dine on food that suits
Its taste for sweet and sticky fruits.

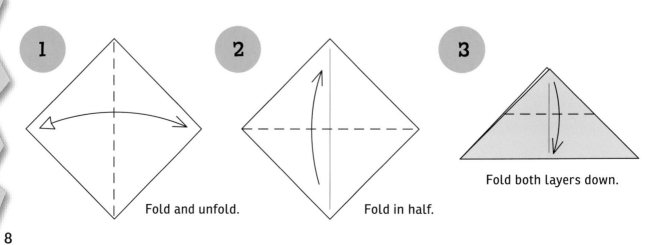

1

Fold and unfold.

2

Fold in half.

3

Fold both layers down.

8

4

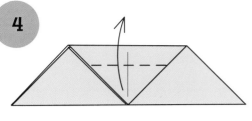

Fold up.

5

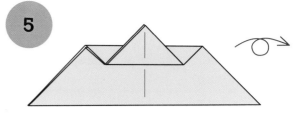

Turn over.

6

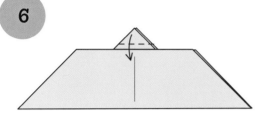

Fold down.

7

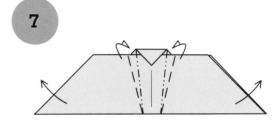

Pleat-fold.

8

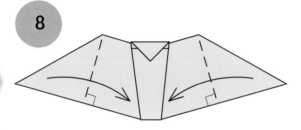

Fold the wings.

9

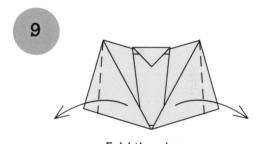

Fold the wings.

10

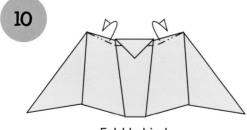

Fold behind.

11

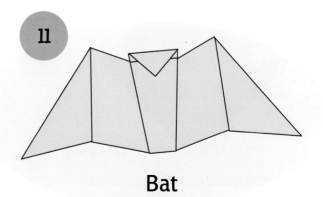

Bat

TOUCAN

Toucan, you can, fit your bill
Like no other ever will.
Rainbow-colored, beaming bright,
Outshining sun and candlelight.
The beak knows best where the bird will go,
And with that schnoz you'll surely know.

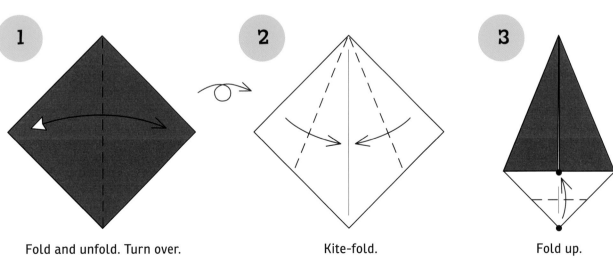

1 Fold and unfold. Turn over.

2 Kite-fold.

3 Fold up.

10

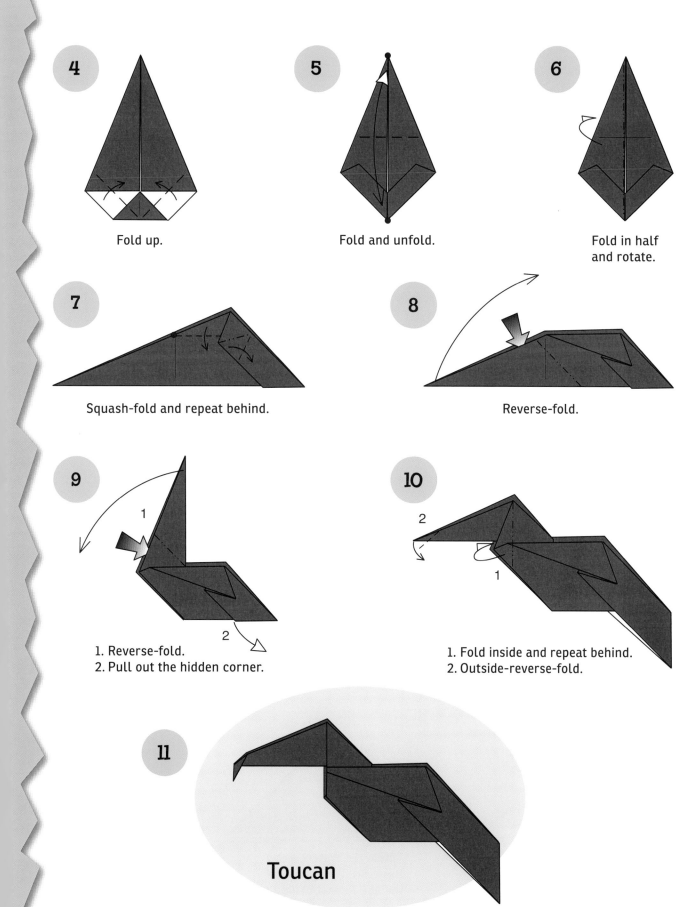

4

Fold up.

5

Fold and unfold.

6

Fold in half
and rotate.

7

Squash-fold and repeat behind.

8

Reverse-fold.

9

1
2

1. Reverse-fold.
2. Pull out the hidden corner.

10

2
1

1. Fold inside and repeat behind.
2. Outside-reverse-fold.

11

Toucan

FROG

Imagine if you were a frog
Perched in a tree or on a log.
What's the first thing you would do?
Hop away or enjoy the view?
Or perhaps you would slyly try
To fling your tongue and snatch up flies.

1

Fold and unfold.
Turn over.

2

Fold and unfold.

3

Collapse along
the creases.

4

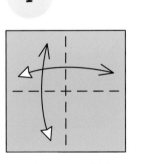

A 3D step.

5

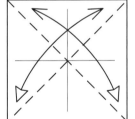

This is the Waterbomb
Base. Bring the edge to
the dot. Repeat behind.

6

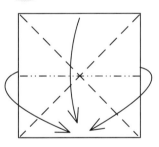

Bring the edge to the
dot. Repeat behind.

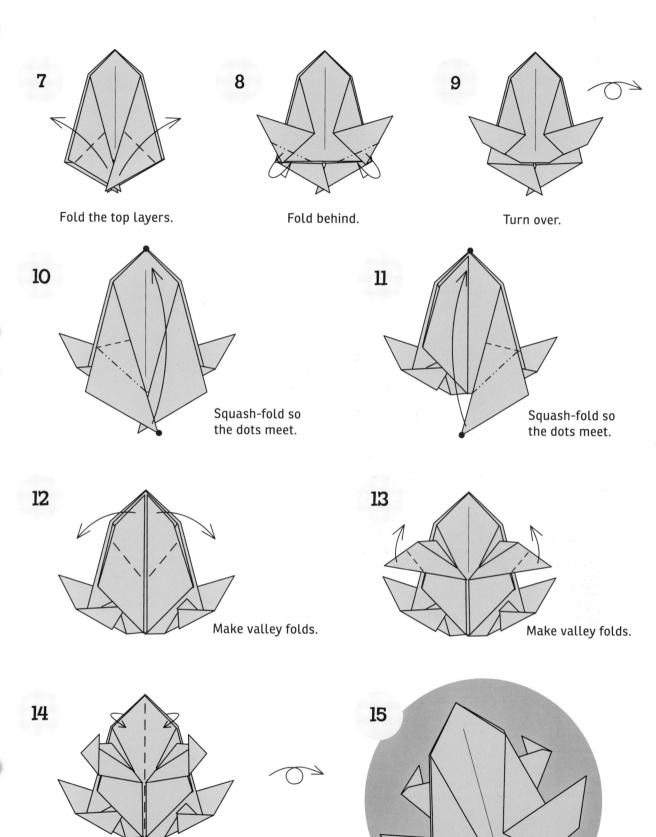

7

Fold the top layers.

8

Fold behind.

9

Turn over.

10

Squash-fold so the dots meet.

11

Squash-fold so the dots meet.

12

Make valley folds.

13

Make valley folds.

14

Bend slightly down the middle to make the Frog 3D. Turn over.

15

Frog

GORILLA

In the jungle rules an ape
Of massive size and hulking shape
Who pounds his chest to prove his might
Over land and beast alike.
So when a drumbeat meets your ear—
Be warned!—a proud gorilla's near.

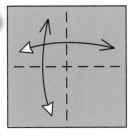

1

Fold and unfold.
Turn over.

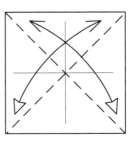

2

Fold and unfold.

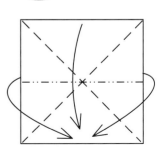

3

Collapse along
the creases.

4

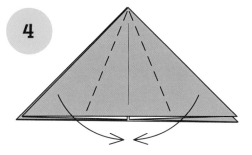

This is the Waterbomb
Base. Fold to the center.

5

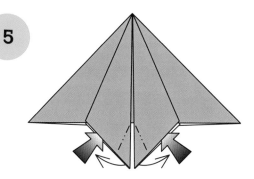

Make reverse folds.

6

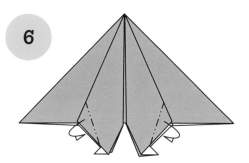

Fold behind.

7

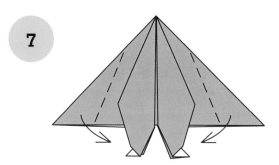

Make valley folds.

8

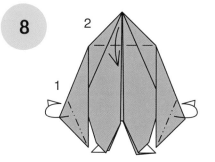

1. Fold behind on
   the left and right.
2. Fold down.

9

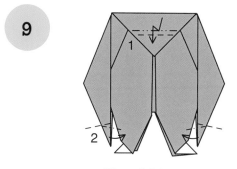

1. Pleat-fold.
2. Make squash folds.

10

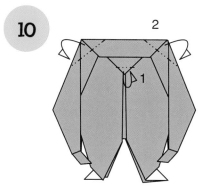

1. Fold behind.
2. Fold behind.

11

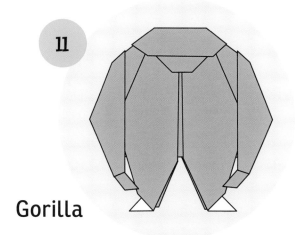

Gorilla

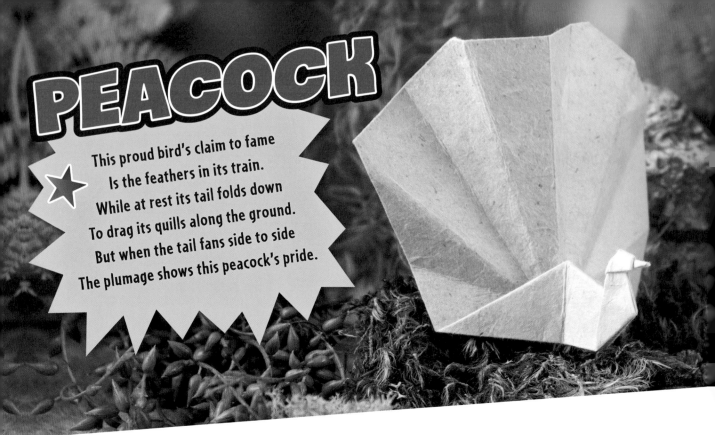

PEACOCK

This proud bird's claim to fame
Is the feathers in its train.
While at rest its tail folds down
To drag its quills along the ground.
But when the tail fans side to side
The plumage shows this peacock's pride.

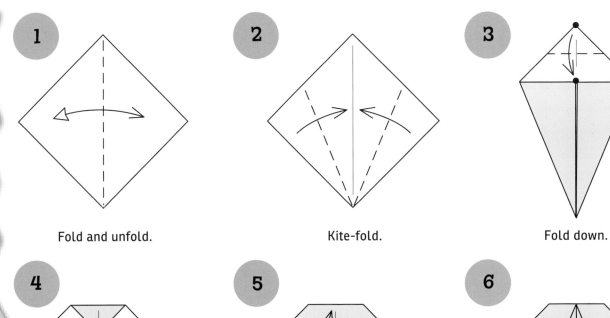

1 Fold and unfold.

2 Kite-fold.

3 Fold down.

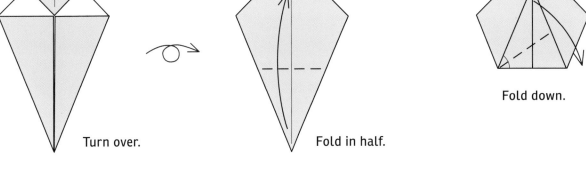

4 Turn over.

5 Fold in half.

6 Fold down.

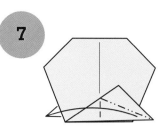

7

Squash-fold.

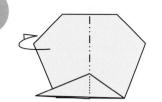

8

Fold behind.

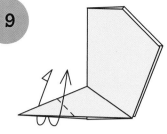

9

Outside-reverse-fold.

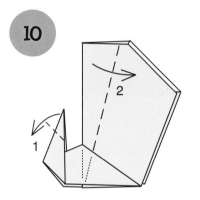

10

1. Outside-reverse-fold.
2. Fold all the layers.

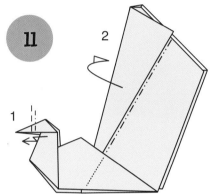

11

1. Crimp-fold.
2. Fold behind.

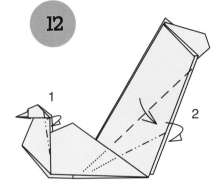

12

1. Fold inside, repeat behind.
2. Pleat-fold.

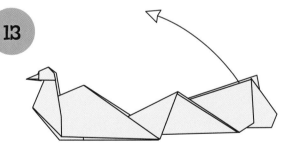

13

Lift and spread the plumes.

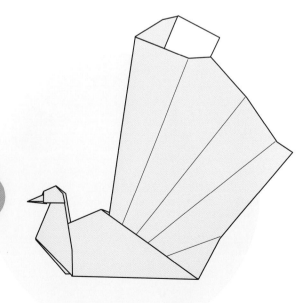

14

Peacock

PARROT

Polly doesn't want a cracker,
And if I were you, I wouldn't ask her.
But if you do, prepare to hear
About those crackers for a year.
For parrots have a special knack
For learning words to repeat back.

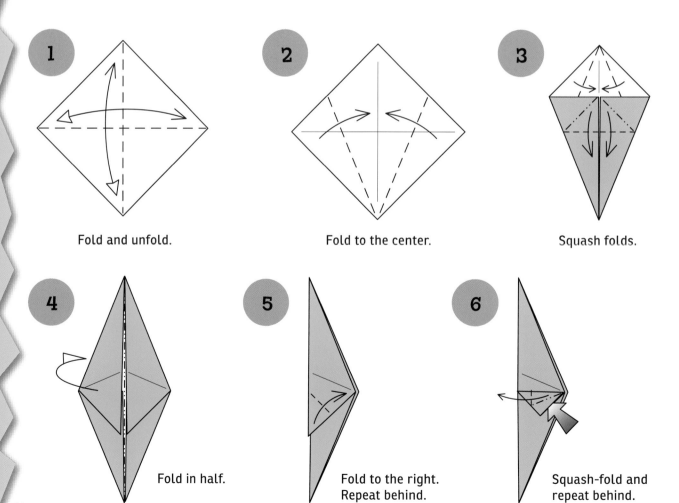

1 Fold and unfold.

2 Fold to the center.

3 Squash folds.

4 Fold in half.

5 Fold to the right. Repeat behind.

6 Squash-fold and repeat behind.

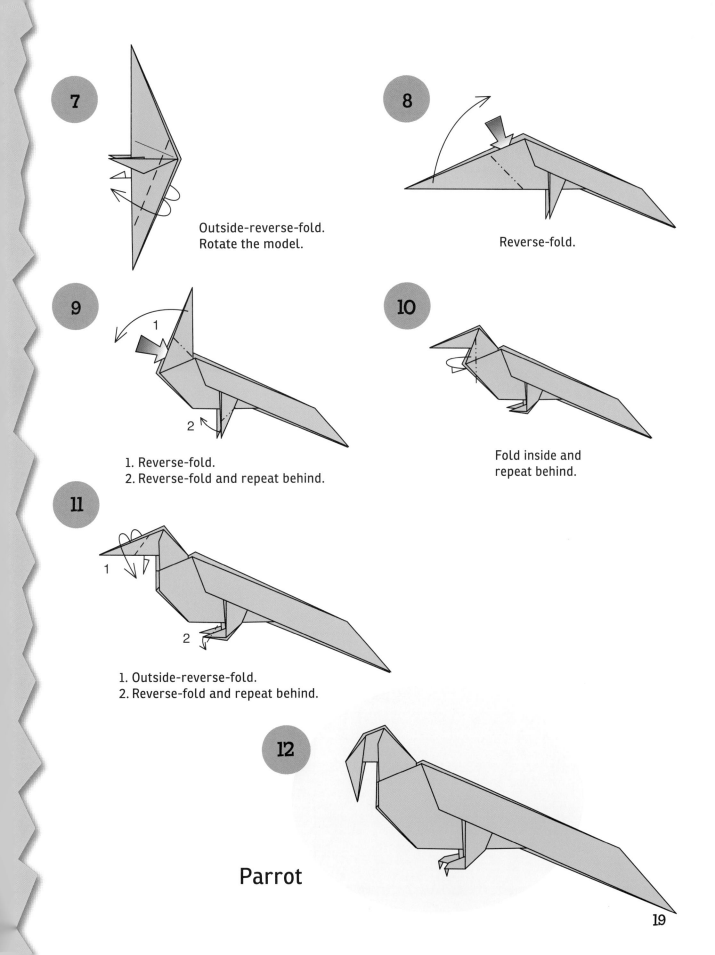

7

Outside-reverse-fold.
Rotate the model.

8

Reverse-fold.

9

1. Reverse-fold.
2. Reverse-fold and repeat behind.

10

Fold inside and
repeat behind.

11

1. Outside-reverse-fold.
2. Reverse-fold and repeat behind.

12

Parrot

CROCODILE

When you sail the river Nile
Beware the hungry crocodile
That swims in silence right beside
The little boat in which you ride.
Whatever you do, don't take a snooze!
For in a snap you'll surely lose!

1

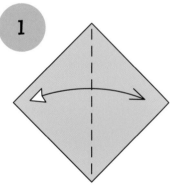

Fold and unfold.

2

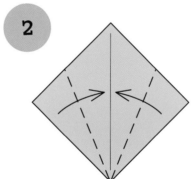

Kite-fold.

3

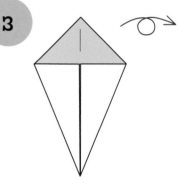

Turn over.

4

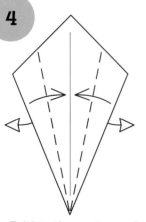

Fold to the center and
swing out from behind.

5

Fold to the center.

6

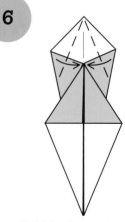

Fold to the center.

20

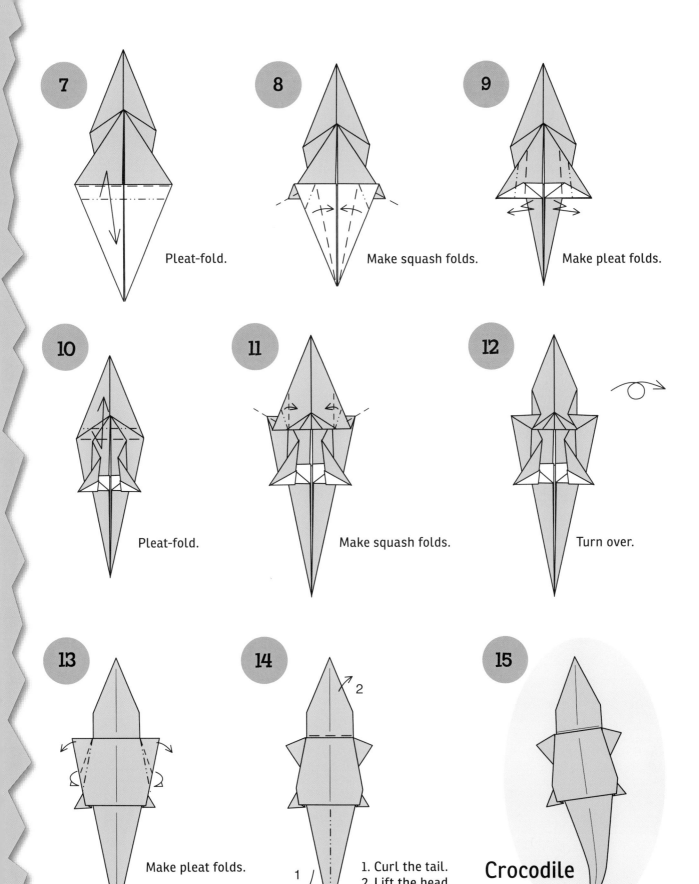

7 Pleat-fold.

8 Make squash folds.

9 Make pleat folds.

10 Pleat-fold.

11 Make squash folds.

12 Turn over.

13 Make pleat folds.

14
1. Curl the tail.
2. Lift the head up a little.

15 Crocodile

21

LION

The mighty lion does not hide
When danger lurks around his pride.
He strides forth and stands up tall
To protect his family—cubs and all.
And seldom does a predator
Stick around to face his roar!

1

Fold and unfold.

2

Fold to the center.

3

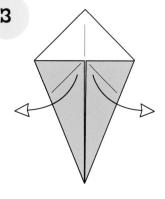

Unfold.

4

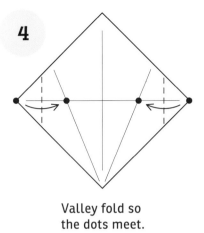

Valley fold so
the dots meet.

5

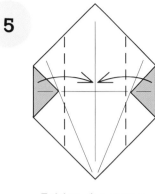

Fold to the center.

6

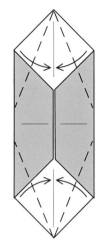

Fold to the center.

7

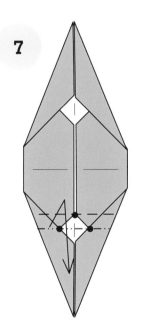

Pleat-fold.

8

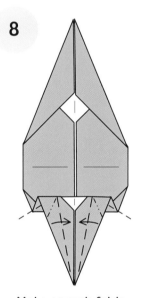

Make squash folds.

9

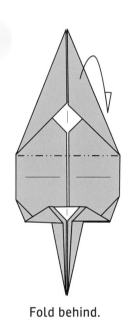

Fold behind.

10

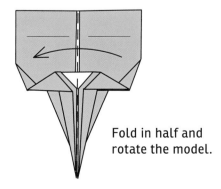

Fold in half and
rotate the model.

11

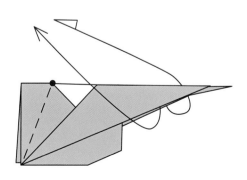

Outside-reverse-fold.

23

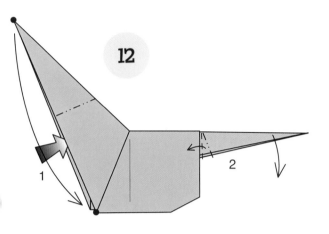

12

1. Reverse-fold so the dots meet.
2. Crimp-fold the tail.

13

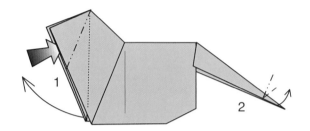

1. Reverse-fold.
2. Crimp-fold the tail.

14

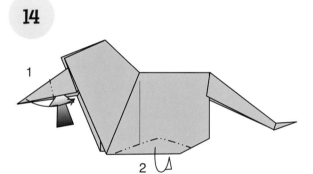

1. Reverse-fold.
2. Shape the legs and body, repeat behind.

15

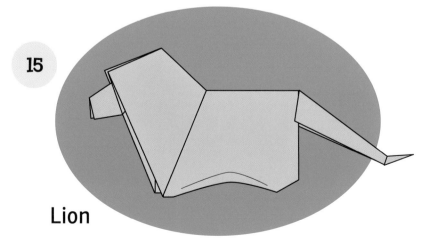

Lion

ELEPHANT

While the jungle creatures slumber
A sneaky elephant softly lumbers
Through the forest, think with vines,
Until the perfect spot she finds.
Then with a trumpeting supreme,
She blasts the sleepers from their dreams.

1

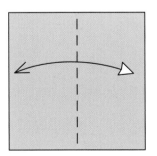

Fold and unfold.

2

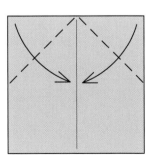

Fold to the center.

3

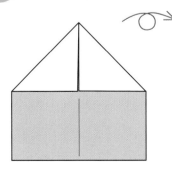

Turn over.

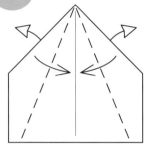

4

Fold to the center and swing out from behind.

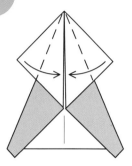

5

Fold to the center.

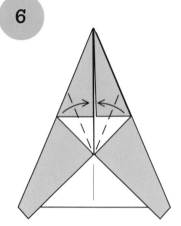

6

Fold to the center.

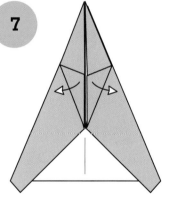

7

Unfold.

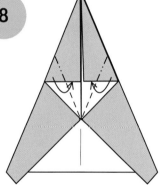

8

Make reverse folds.

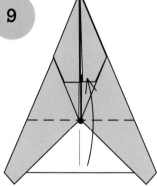

9

Fold up and under the ears.

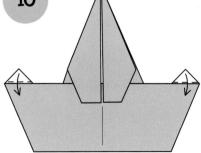

10

Fold down.

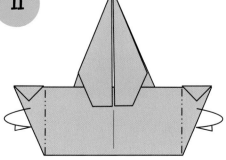

11

Fold behind.

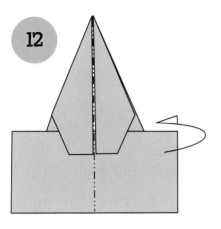

12

Fold in half and
rotate the model.

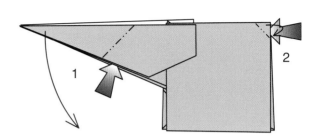

13

1. Reverse-fold.
2. Reverse-fold.

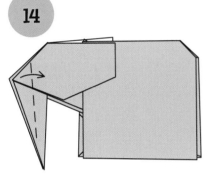

14

Valley-fold and
repeat behind.

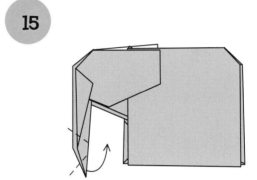

15

Shape the trunk
with reverse folds.

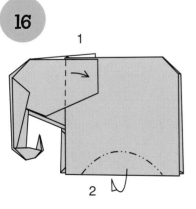

16

1. Fold the ears out a little.
2. Shape the legs and body.
   Repeat behind.

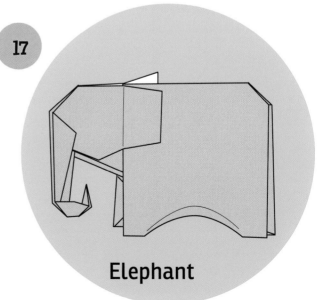

17

Elephant

FLAMINGO

You don't need fancy words or lingo
To describe the fair flamingo.
A long, curved neck. A black-tipped beak.
Tall, thin legs with small webbed feet.
But best of all—I truly think—
Are its feathers—flaming pink!

1

Fold and unfold.

2

Kite-fold.

3

Unfold.

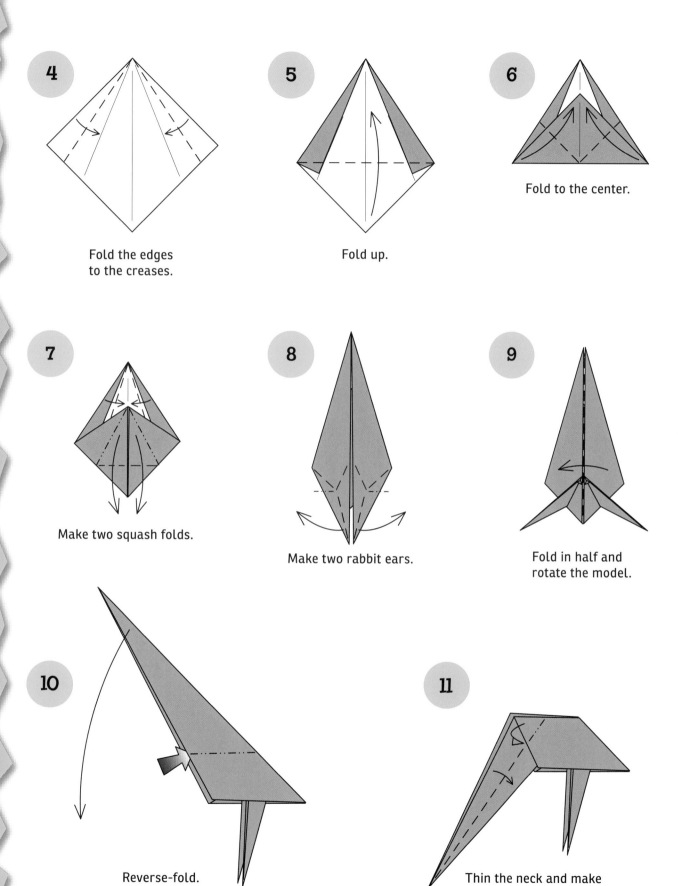

4 Fold the edges to the creases.

5 Fold up.

6 Fold to the center.

7 Make two squash folds.

8 Make two rabbit ears.

9 Fold in half and rotate the model.

10 Reverse-fold.

11 Thin the neck and make a reverse fold at the top. Repeat behind.

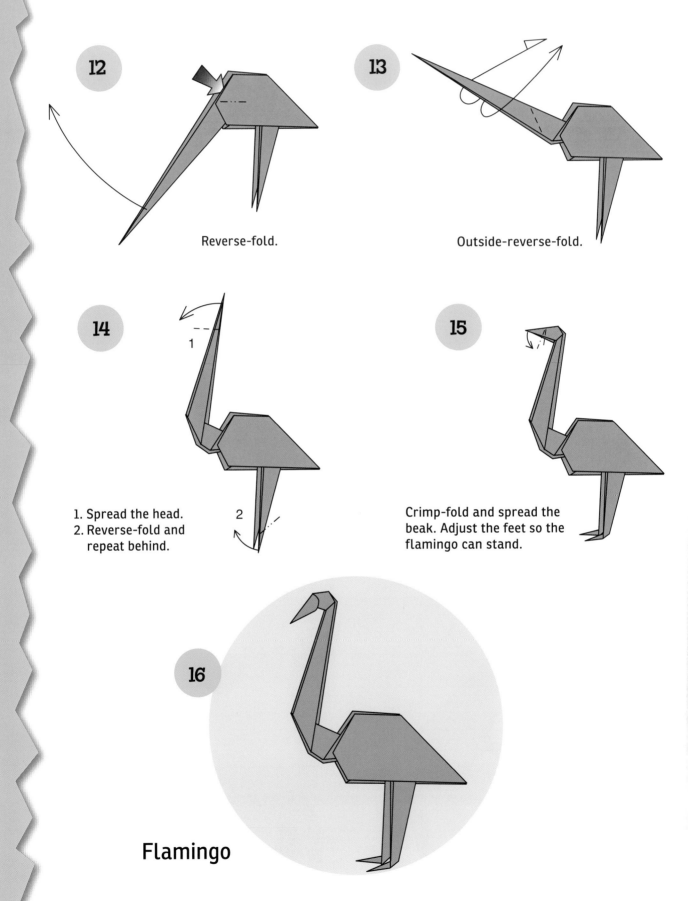

12

Reverse-fold.

13

Outside-reverse-fold.

14

1
2

1. Spread the head.
2. Reverse-fold and
   repeat behind.

15

Crimp-fold and spread the
beak. Adjust the feet so the
flamingo can stand.

16

Flamingo

Read More

Azzità, Emanuele. *Origami Birds.* Exciting Origami. New York: Enslow Publishing, 2018.

Harbo, Christopher. *Easy Origami Greeting Cards.* Origami Crafting in 4D. North Mankato, Minn.: Capstone Press, 2017.

Hardyman, Robyn. *Jungle Animals.* Origami Fun. Minneapolis: Bellwether Media, Inc., 2018.

Owen, Ruth. *Jungle Animals.* Origami Safari. New York: Windmill Books, 2015.

Internet Sites

Use FactHound to find Internet sites related to this book.

Visit *www.facthound.com*

Just type in 9781543513066 and go.

Makerspace Tips

Download tips and tricks for using this book and others in a library makerspace.

Visit www.capstonepub.com/dabblelabresources

Dabble Lab Books are published by Capstone Press
1710 Roe Crest Drive, North Mankato, Minnesota 56003
www.mycapstone.com

Library of Congress Cataloging-in-Publication Data is
available at the Library of Congress website.
ISBN: 978-1-5435-1306-6 (library hardcover)
ISBN: 978-1-5435-1310-3 (eBook PDF)

Editorial Credits
Christopher Harbo, editor; Lori Bye, designer;
Morgan Walters, media researcher; Kathy McColley,
production specialist

Photo Credits
Capstone Studio/Karon Dubke, all photos;
John Montroll, all diagrams

Printed and bound in the USA. PA021

John Montroll is respected for his work in origami throughout the
world. He started folding in elementary school and quickly progressed
from folding models from books to creating his own designs. Today,
John has written and published many books, and each origami model
that he designs has a meticulously developed folding sequence. The
American origami master is known for being the inspiration behind
the single-square, no cuts, no glue approach in origami, and his
long-standing experience allows him to accomplish a model in fewer
steps, rather than more. It is John's constant goal to give the reader a
pleasing folding experience.